THE
DISEASE OF THE
HEALTH & WEALTH
GOSPELS

THE
DISEASE OF THE
HEALTH & WEALTH
GOSPELS

GORDON D. FEE

REGENT COLLEGE PUBLISHING
Vancouver, British Columbia

The Disease of the Health and Wealth Gospels
Copyright © 1985, 2006 by Gordon D. Fee
All rights reserved

First edition published 1985 by Frontline Publishing

This edition published 2006 by
Regent College Publishing
5800 University Boulevard, Vancouver, BC V6T 2E4 Canada
www.regentpublishing.com

Views expressed in works published by Regent College Publishing
are those of the author and do not necessarily represent the official
position of Regent College <www.regent-college.edu>.

Library and Archives Canada Cataloguing in Publication

Fee, Gordon D.
The disease of the health and wealth gospels / Gordon D. Fee.

Includes bibliographical references.
ISBN 1-57383-066-6

1. Health—Biblical teaching. 2. Wealth—Biblical teaching.
I. Title.

BT732.F43 2006   261.8'321   C2006-901200-8

CONTENTS

1

THE 'GOSPEL' OF PROSPERITY

Amerian Christianity is rapidly being infected by an
insidious disease, the so called wealth and health
Gospel—although it has very little of the character of
Gospel in it.

In its more brazen forms (Brother Al, Reverend Ike, etc.) it
simply says, "Serve God and get rich (or be healthy)." In its more
respectable, but more pernicious forms, it builds 15-million-dol-
lar crystal cathedrals to the glory of affluent suburban Christianity. Or it says, "God wills your prosperity (and health)."

The message goes like this: "It's in the Bible. God says it. So
think God's thoughts. Claim it. And it's yours!"

I recognize that not all adherents of this currently fashionable
gospel say or do it so boldly, and that the two (wealth and health)
can be avowed separately; but the biblical and theological distortions that lie behind both are similar. Indeed, the theology of this
new "gospel" seems far more to fit the American dream than it
does the teaching of Him who had "nowhere to lay His head."

In this present paper l am addressing myself only to the matter
of prosperity; and it should be noted at the outset that this is not

a personal attack on anyone. On the contrary, I am convinced that many of the better-known figures in this movement—e.g., Oral Roberts, Kenneth and Gloria Copeland, Kenneth Hagen, Robert Schuller—are not devious people out to get rich at the expense of others. Nonetheless their message is in fact a dangerous twisting of God's truth, a message which can appeal ultimately only to human fallenness, not to our life in the Spirit.

The problems are both biblical and theological. So first a look at their use of Scripture.

1. The basic problem with the cult of prosperity lies right at the point which the evangelists themselves consider to be their strength—the interpretation of Scripture. Indeed, much that is said by them has a biblical ring to it, which is precisely why so many well-meaning people fall into the trap. Thus Oral Roberts, for example, repeatedly reminds people that putting material things ahead of God is sinful;[1] and Robert Schuller rightly argues that God loves the affluent as well as the poor. In his *The Laws of Prosperity*, Kenneth Copeland says, among other things: Money, although not evil in itself, makes a "lousy god"; true prosperity is spiritual as well as financial; prosperity should not be an end in itself, but a means of helping others; one should take God at His Word, and trust Him. These, and many other things, are truly said; who can fault them?

The fault, of course, lies not with such isolated truths, but with the bottom line, which always comes back to one continual reaffirmation: God *wills* the (financial) prosperity of every one of his children, and therefore for a Christian to be in poverty is to be outside God's intended will;

1. See, e.g., *God Is a Good God* (Indianapolis: Bobbs-Merrill, 1960), pp. 58-64.

it is to be living a Satan-defeated life. And usually tucked away in this affirmation is a second: Because we are God's children (the King's kids, as some like to put it) we should always go first-class—we should have the biggest and best, a Cadillac instead of a Volkswagen, because this alone brings glory to God (a curious theology indeed, given the nature of the Incarnation and the Crucifixion). But these affirmations are *not* biblical, no matter how much one might clothe them in biblical garb. The basic problems here are hermeneutical; i.e., they involve questions as to how one interprets Scripture. Even the lay person, who may not know the word "hermeneutics" and who is not especially trained in interpreting the Bible, senses that this is where the real problem lies.

The most distressing thing about their use of Scripture, to use Copeland's book as an example, is the purely subjective and arbitrary way they interpret the biblical text. Copeland, of course, argues just the opposite, but the evidence speaks for itself. On his first page (p. 13), he tells us "that we are putting the Word of God first and foremost throughout this study, not what we *think* it says, but what it *actually* says!" (italics and exclamation his). This is nobly said; but what does it mean? Implied is the hint that interpretations that differ from his are based on what people think, not on what the Bible says. But also implied is the truth that good interpretation should begin with the plain meaning of the text.

The *plain meaning* of the text, however, is precisely what Copeland and the others do not give us, text after text. Let it be understood that the plain meaning of the text is *always* the first rule, as well as the ultimate goal, of all valid interpretation. But "plain meaning" has first of all to do with the author's original *intent,* it has to do with what would have been plain to those to

9

whom the words were originally addressed. It has *not* to do with how someone from a suburbanized white American culture of the late 20th century reads his own cultural setting back into the text through the frequently distorted prism of the language of the early 17th century.

L et us take, for example, the "basic Scripture text" of this movement (3 John 2, in the King James Version): "Beloved, I wish above all things that thou mayest prosper and be in health, even as thy soul prospereth." Of this text Copeland says, "John writes that we *should* prosper and be in health" (p. 14). But is this what the text *actually* says? Hardly!

In the first place, the Greek word translated "prosper" in the KJV means "to go well with someone," just as a friend in a letter two days ago said, "I pray that this letter finds you all well" (cf. 3 John 2 in the KJV, GNB, NEB, RSV, etc.). This combination of wishing for "things to go well" and for the recipient's "good health" was the *standard* form of greeting in a personal letter in antiquity.[2] To extend John's wish for Gaius to refer to financial and material prosperity for all Christians of all times is *totally foreign* to the text. John neither intended that, nor could Gaius have so understood it. Thus it cannot be the "plain meaning" of the text.

We may rightly learn from this text to pray for our brothers and sisters that "all will go well with them"; but to argue from the text that God wills our financial prosperity is to abuse the text, not use it. One may well argue that all subsequent Christians are out of God's will who do not go to Carpus's house in Troy in order to take Paul's cloak to him (2 Tim. 4:13), or that all Christians with

2. See, e.g., the collection of ancient personal letters in the Loeb series: A.S. Hunt and C.C. Edgar, eds., *Select Papyri* (New York: Putnam, 1932), pp. 269-395.

stomach ailments are not to pray for healing at all, but rather to stop drinking water and to drink wine instead (1 Tim. 5:23). For these, too, are what the texts *actually say*, in Copeland's sense.

It should be noted further that "abundant life" in John 10:10, the second important text of this movement, also has nothing to do with material abundance. "Life" or "eternal life" in John's Gospel is the equivalent of the "Kingdom of God" in the Synoptics. It literally means the "life of the Age to Come." It is the life that God has in and of Himself; and it is his gift to believers in the present age.[3] The Greek word *perrison*, translated "more abundantly" in the KJV, means simply that believers are to enjoy this gift of life to the full" (NIV). Material abundance is not implied either in the word "life" or "to the full." Furthermore, such an idea is totally foreign to the context of John 10, as well as to the whole of the teaching of Jesus.

Beyond these misunderstandings of the "basic texts" there are several examples, in Copeland's book especially, where he simply runs roughshod over the plain meaning of texts—because the plain meaning so clearly runs counter to his invalid interpretations of the basic texts. At such points his "interpretation" is said to come from the "Holy Spirit." But what Copeland does to the story of the "rich young ruler" (pp. 62-63)—suggesting that Jesus is affirming his wealth as the result of his lifelong obedience, and was only testing him to give it away, so that he might regain all the more—is so plainly contrary to the *intent* of the text that he would do well to be careful about attributing to the Holy Spirit *that* bit of subjectivity. Otherwise, the Holy Spirit, who inspired

---

3. Cf. C.K. Barrett, *The Gospel According to St. John* (2nd ed.; Philadelphia: Westminster, 1978), pp. 214-15.

the original text with its plain meaning, is now to be found contradicting Himself.

Copeland's (and his friends') hermeneutics therefore is not in fact attempting to give us only what the Bible actually says. It is almost totally subjective, and comes not from study but from "meditation," which in Copeland's case means a kind of free association based on a prior commitment to his—totally wrong—understanding of the "basic" texts.

2. It should be noted further that this "gospel" is also not biblical in the larger sense of that word, in that it reflects a truncated view of the whole of Scripture. The selectivity of these evangelists allows them not only to espouse a view *not taught anywhere in the New Testament,* but also carefully to avoid hundreds of texts that stand squarely in opposition to their teaching.

This hermeneutical selectivity is most noticeable in their understanding of poverty and prosperity, which they themselves see as the conflicting realities. Thus it is often argued that the "traditional" Christian view is that prosperity is evil, and therefore that God would prefer us to be in poverty. Against this they argue that poverty is a curse (from Deut. 28:15 ff.), and therefore *not* in God's will, whereas prosperity is His will. This is further supported by "conventional wisdom," which fails to take seriously both the nature of the Fall and the reality of common grace.

Conventional wisdom sees life always in terms of *quid pro quo,* one thing in return for another. For every evil, there is a direct, specific cause ("Who sinned, this man or his parents, that he was born blind?"; Job's comforters; etc.). And for every good, especially every material blessing, there is also a direct specific cause. Some "rules" that God has laid down are being followed.

12

But conventional wisdom is *not* biblical. Even though there are special times when God does protect His own, it is clear from the whole of Scripture that *both* the sun *and* the rain fall on the just and the unjust alike. The Galileans whom Pilate killed and the eighteen on whom the tower fell were not greater sinners, Jesus said (Luke 13:1-5). Conventional wisdom is simply *not* true. The Fall has so permeated the created order that all people are affected by its consequences, and God has revealed Himself as abounding in mercy-even to the sinner. Sometimes there seems to be no good reason why the wicked are "blessed" while the good are not, or *vice versa!*

Furthermore, even though God has promised the vindication of His own, He has seldom promised immediate vindication. For example, in Hebrews 11:32-39, some by faith saw great victories; but others *by faith were destitute.* But they are *all* commended for their faith. And these words were spoken to encourage believers who themselves had "joyfully accepted the confiscation of their property" (10:34 NIV), but who were now about to lose heart. Immediate vindication, however, is not promised to them, only eschatological (10:35-36). Conventional wisdom, therefore, cannot be made a part of the biblical view of poverty and prosperity.

I n the full biblical view, wealth and possessions are a zero value for the people of God. Granted that often in the Old Testament—but *never* in the New—possessions are frequently related to a life of obedience. But even here they are seen to have the inherent double danger of removing the eye from trusting God and of coming to possess the possessor. Poverty, however, is *not* seen to be better. If God has revealed Himself as the One who pleads the cause of the poor—and He

13

has throughout Scripture—He is not thereby blessing poverty. Rather, He is revealing His mercy and justice in behalf of those whom the wealthy regularly oppress in order to get, or maintain, their wealth.

This carefree attitude toward wealth and possessions, for which *neither* prosperity *nor* poverty is a value, is thoroughgoing in the New Testament. According to Jesus, the good news of the inbreaking of the Kingdom frees us from all those pagan concerns (Matt. 6:32). With His own coming the Kingdom has been inaugurated-even though it has yet to be fully consummated; the time of God's rule is now; the future with its new values is already at work in the present. We have been "seized" by the Kingdom; our old values, the old way of looking at things, is on the way out; we are joyously freed from the tyranny of all other lords. In the new order, brought about by Jesus, the standard is sufficiency, and surplus is called into question. The one with two tunics should share with him who has none (Luke 3:11); "possessions" are to be sold and given to the poor (Luke 12:33). Indeed, in the new age *unshared wealth* is contrary to the Kingdom breaking in as good news to the poor. Therefore, if one has possessions (precisely because they have no inherent value) he can freely share them with the needy. But if one does not have possessions, he is not to seek them. God cares for one's needs; the extras are unnecessary The rich man who seeks more and more is a fool; life does not consist in having a surplus of possessions (Luke 12:15).

It is precisely this new age attitude that one finds reflected in the early chapters of the Acts. The early church was *not* communal. But they were the new community—the new people of God. Hence no one considers anything owned to be his or her own possession. The coming of the Spirit that marked the beginning of the new order had freed them from the need of possessing. Hence there was sufficiency, and no one was in need.

This same carefree attitude toward wealth and possessions also marks all of Paul. He is a free man in Christ, who knows contentment whatever the circumstances. He knows both want and plenty, both hunger and being well fed. He "can do all things"—which in this context clearly refers to being in need!"—through Christ who gives [him] strength" (Phil. 4: 10-13).

Thus he tells those who have nothing to be content with food and clothing. "People *who want to get* rich fall into temptation and a trap" (1 Tim. 6:6-10). But then he remembers those who *happen to be rich*. They are to treat their wealth with indifference; they must not put any stock in it. Rather they are to be "generous and willing to share," for this is true wealth (6:17-19). The point is in the New Age, prosperity is simply no value at all. How, then, can God will such a zero value for all His children?

The cult of prosperity thus flies full in the face of the whole New Testament. It is not biblical *in any* sense.

3. Finally, besides being non-biblical, the *theology* that lies behind this perversion of the Gospel is sub-Christian at several crucial points. Since that requires another whole article of its own, I will here only briefly note several of the more readily observable theological weaknesses.

First, despite all protests to the contrary, at its base the cult of prosperity offers a man-centered, rather than a God-centered, theology. Even though one is regularly told that it is to God's own glory that we should prosper, the appeal is always made to our own selfishness and sense of well-being. In fact, the only one who could possibly believe this non-biblical nonsense is someone who wants to, and the only reason one would want to is because of its appeal to one's selfishness. Many years ago, writing of God's holiness, Gustav Aulen warned:[4]

> Holiness stands as a sentinel against all eudaemonistic and anthropocentric interpretations of religion. Holiness meets us as unconditional majesty. Every attempt to transform Christian faith into a religion of satisfaction and enjoyment is thereby doomed to failure. Egocentricity masquerading in the robes of religion is excluded. Faith in God cannot be measured and evaluated from the point of view of human happiness and needs, even if these concepts be even so refined and "spiritualized." God is not someone faith employs with an eye to the higher or lower advantages which he may be able to furnish; nor is he someone we can call upon in order that our needs and desires may be met. Even if anthropocentricity should disguise itself in the most clever costume, it will inevitably be unmasked by the Holy One. Every tendency to make God serve human interests is irrevocably doomed.

He goes on: "If God is the Holy One, he is also the One on whom we are 'absolutely dependent.' We are in his power, not he in ours." And the whole creation should respond: "Amen."

Second, this false gospel presents a totally false theology of giving. In the New Testament, as well as the Old, God's love and giving are predicated on His mercy, and therefore in their every expression they are unconditional. Cod loves, and gives, and forgives unconditionally—no strings attached. The human response to divine grace is gratitude, which expresses itself in identical, unconditional love, and giving, and forgiving. The cult of prosperity, on the other hand, tells us we are to give in order to get. It is by giving to the Lord, and to the poor, Copeland assures us, that we are guaranteeing our own prosperity. Furthermore, he candidly admits that he will give to the poor *only* on the condition that

4. *The Faith of the Christian Church* (London: SCM, 1960), p. 105.

he is also given opportunity to tell them about Jesus. As noble as that end might sound, the means to the end is manipulative. It is evangelism tied to the apron strings of the American profit-motive mentality.

Third, such an Americanized perversion of the Gospel tends to reinforce a way of life and an economic system that repeatedly oppresses the poor—the very thing that the prophetic message denounces so forcefully. Seeking more prosperity in an already affluent society means to support all the political and economic programs that have made such prosperity available—but almost always at the expense of economically deprived individuals and nations.

The best antidote to this disease, therefore, is a good healthy dose of biblical theology. For an excellent exposition of the biblical view of wealth and poverty, as well as for some helpful suggestions toward a truly Christian response to the needs of the poor, I recommend Ronald J. Sider's *Rich Christians in an Age of Hunger*.[5] This book should be *must* reading for every American Christian. In some ways it is tough medicine, but it should help to cure this loathsome disease. And in this case, I would be so bold and prophetic as to declare that the only alternative to such a "cure" is the awful judgment of God, which must begin first with the house of God.

One may count on it: Any "Gospel" that will not "sell" as well among believers in Ouagadougou, Burkina Faso or Dacca, Bangladesh or Phnom Penh, Cambodia as in Orange County, California or Tulsa County, Oklahoma *is not* the Gospel of our Lord Jesus Christ.

---

5. Published by Intervarsity Press, 1977.

2

THE 'GOSPEL' OF
PERFECT HEALTH

The second part of the "wealth and health Gospel," that God wills our perfect health, differs from the cult of prosperity in several significant ways. In the first place, the physical and mental healing of human life *is* part of the redemptive activity of God. In contrast to the cult of prosperity, the "gospel" of perfect health is a distortion of something which in fact is biblical, since the New Testament stands squarely on the side of healing: It is part of Jesus' and the apostles' ministries; gifts of healing are part of the church's *charismata*; and at least one text (James 5:14-15) specifically enjoins believers to pray for the sick with the promise of answered prayer.

Furthermore, whereas material possessions are irrelevant to the people of God (they freely give if they have them, but they do not seek them), the same is not true of the human body. At least one of the reasons Christians pray for the sick to be healed is their conviction that the body, though still subject to decay and death in the present age, nonetheless belongs to the Lord and is destined for resurrection (1 Corinthians 6:13-14). A body healed—or healthy—because of God's gracious activity in our behalf is a sign of the future already at work in the present age.

If this is true, that both Scripture and theology support our praying in faith for the gracious healing of the sick, then wherein lies the problem? What is the "disease" nature of the "gospel" of total health for Christians? Basically, it lies in some biblical and theological distortions which insist: (1) that God wills perfect health and complete healing for every believer, and (2) that God has obligated Himself to heal every sickness for those who have faith (unless the sickness is the result of breaking God's "health" laws). Integral to this theology is the insistence that faith can *claim* such healing from God, and that any failure to be healed is not the fault of God but of the one who has not had enough faith. Very often *claiming* healing means to *confess* it as done, even though the symptoms persist, so that at times one meets a blind, or diseased, person who claims to have been healed, even though the blind continue to grope in darkness and the sick still are riddled with pain.

Since I am obviously on the side of miraculous healing, I hesitate to try to combat this distortion, lest I sound like one who is against it altogether. But not so. I firmly believe that gifts of healing belong in the church. But I also believe that this over-zealous attempt to bring glory to God is in fact a distortion of truth that has created a number of neurotic believers (because they don't seem to be able to muster up "enough faith"), and has kept the church as a whole from being open to the gift of healing. Therefore, although my sympathies lie with the evangelists here, I must protest the bad biblical interpretation and theology of this movement.

As with many such half-truths, the "gospel" of perfect health seeks (commendably) to base itself entirely on Scripture. However, the use of Scripture by evangelists of this gospel is faulty in precisely the same three ways as with the wealth side of their "gospel": (1) some poor, or flat-out wrong, interpretations of key texts, (2) selective use of texts, and (3) failure to have a wholistic biblical view of things, especially a failure to understand the essential theological framework of the New Testament writers. As a result, they tend to repeat the Corinthian error and are unable to hear Paul's answers in 1 and 2 Corinthians as over against themselves—although these evangelists are the unwitting descendants of the false apostles of 2 Corinthians 10-13.

1. As noted in the previous article, the aim of all biblical interpretation is the "plain meaning" of the text. What is meant by this, of course, is the *original* meaning, that meaning which the author *plainly* intended and that the original readers should have *plainly* understood. Although the Bible is indeed a book for all seasons, and speaks out of the past directly to our present situation, it does so because it *first* spoke to them in their situation. Therefore, the first task of interpretation is *not* to find out what it says to us, but to find out what it originally said to them. God's Word to us is not a new word, never before discovered; rather it must be the very same word that He originally spoke back then and there. And this is the only legitimate Word to be heard in Scripture.

All of this must be insisted upon because the basic biblical failure of the "perfect health" evangelists is the interpretation of their primary texts. They simply fail to do adequate *exegesis,* which has to do with determining the meaning of a text in its original context.

The arguments for full and complete health as God's only will for all believers are based on three sets of texts: a) Paul's statement that "Christ redeemed us from the curse of the law" (Galatians 3:14) coupled with Deuteronomy 28:21-22, where disease is one of the curses of disobedience to the law. It is argued from these texts that sickness is a part of the "curse of the law" from which Christ redeemed us. b) Isaiah 53 and the citation of 53:4 in Matthew and of 53:5 in 1 Peter 2:24. It is argued from these texts, and especially from the change to the past tense in 1 Peter, that healing is in the atonement in the same way as forgiveness. c) A whole host of texts that remind us that God honors faith; e.g., Matthew 9:29; Mark 11:23-24; John 14:12; Hebrews 11:6; James 1:6-8.

Space does not allow a thorough investigation of all these texts, but a few suggestions are in order.

a) The first set of texts may be quickly set aside. This is a typical example of a totally faulty "concordance" interpretation, which finds English catch words in various texts and then tries to make them all refer to the same thing. There is not even the remotest possibility that Paul was referring to the "curses" of Deuteronomy 28 when he spoke of the "curse of the law." And "redemption" in Galatians has to do with one thing only: how does one have rightstanding with God—through faith (= trust in God's gracious acceptance and forgiveness of sinners), or by works of the law (=acceptance by obedience to prescribed rules)? Thus the Holy Spirit could scarcely have inspired a meaning of the text that is

22

so totally foreign to the point Paul is making in this context in Galatians.

b) It is also questionable whether one can rightly argue that the Bible teaches that healing is provided for in the atonement. Such a doctrine has in fact been the position of historic Pentecostalism. However, the "position paper" on divine healing adopted by the General Presbytery of the Assemblies of God (dated August 20, 1974) makes it quite clear that the historic position does not see healing in the atonement in the same way as salvation. Healing is "provided for" because the "atonement brought release from the . . . consequences of sin"; nonetheless, since "we have not yet received the redemption of our bodies," suffering and death are still our lot until the resurrection.

I t would seem, therefore, that only in a circuitous way is it really possible to argue for bodily healing in the atonement. While there are scores of texts that explicitly tell us that our sin has been overcome through Christ's death and resurrection, there is *no* text that explicitly says the same about healing, not even Isaiah 53 and its New Testament citations.

Matthew's use of Isaiah 53:4 does not even refer to the cross; rather he clearly sees the text as being fulfilled in Jesus' *earthly ministry*. This is made certain both by the context and by his choice of Greek verbs in his own unique translation of the Hebrew *(elaben=* he took; *ebastasen* = he removed).

The citation of Isaiah 53:5 in 1 Peter, on the other hand, does not refer to physical healing. The usage here is metaphorical, pure and simple. In a context in which slaves are urged to submit to their evil masters—even if it means their suffering for it—Peter appeals to the example of Christ, which Christian slaves are to follow. This appeal to Christ, beginning at verse 21, is filled with allusions to and citations of Isaiah 53, all of which refer to Christ's having suffered unjustly as the source of the slave's redemption from sin. Thus Peter says: "He himself bore our sins (Isaiah 53:12, cf. 53:4 in the Septuagint)... that we might die to sin." He then goes on: "By his wounds you have been healed (53:5), *for* you were as sheep going astray (53:6)." The allusions to both verses 5 and 6, joined by *for* and referring to "sheep going astray," plus the change to the past tense, all make it abundantly clear that "healing" here is a metaphor for being restored to health from the sickness of their sins. Such a metaphorical usage would be natural for Peter, since sin as "wound," "injury" or "sickness" and the "healing" of such "sickness" are thoroughgoing images in the Old Testament (see, e.g., 2 Chronicles 7:14; Psalm 6:2; Isaiah 1:5-6; Jeremiah 30:12-13, 51:8-9; Nahum 3:19). Furthermore, the Old Testament citations in 1Peter rather closely follow the Septuagint (the pre-Christian Greek translation of the Old Testament), even when this translation differs from the Hebrew; and the Septuagint had *already* translated Isaiah 53:4 metaphorically ("He himself bore our sins," rather than "our sickness").

My point: Matthew clearly saw Isaiah 53:4 as referring to *physical healing,* but as a part of the Messiah's ministry, not as a part of the atonement. Peter, conversely, saw the "healing" in Isaiah 53 as being metaphorical and thus referring to the healing of our *sin* sickness. Thus *neither* New Testament reference sees the "healing" of Isaiah 53 as referring to *physical healing in the atonement.* But what did Isaiah himself intend? Almost certainly his first reference is metaphorical, as the Septuagint, the Targums, and Peter all recognize. Israel was diseased; she was grievously wounded for her sins (Isaiah 1:6-7). Yet God would restore His people. There would come one who himself would suffer so as to deliver. In grand cadences of Hebrew poetry (note the synonymous parallelism), Isaiah says of him: "The *punishment* that brought us peace was upon him, and by his *wounds* we are *healed.*" In the context of Isaiah, that refers first of all to the healing of the wounds and disease of sin. Yet, since physical disease was clearly recognized to be a consequence of the Fall, such a metaphor could also carry with it the *literal* sense, and this is what Matthew picked up.

The Bible, therefore, does not explicitly teach that healing is provided for in the atonement. However, the New Testament does see the cross as the focus of God's redemptive activity. In this sense (and in the sense that sickness is ultimately a result of the Fall), one may perhaps argue that healing also finds its focal point in the atonement.

c) The "faith" passages are in fact the crucial ones for the total health movement. After all, other Christians have used the two previous sets of texts as a biblical basis for healing. The argument for perfect health, or healing on demand, lies finally in the joining of healing as a part of the atonement (the basis of the demand: God has provided for it, therefore He must heal when asked) with all the texts on faith (since it is fully provided for by God, it may be secured by the correct formula of faith). Thus the great emphasis in this movement is on "raising peoples' faith."

We cannot here examine all these texts. But a few words are in order. First, not all the texts frequently cited by the evangelists refer to faith in God for the miraculous. Nonetheless, several of them clearly do (e.g., Mark

11:22-24; James 5:14-15), and a restoration of these texts into the life of the church is not a totally bad thing. In fact, these texts on faith have regularly been a bit of an embarrassment to the church. They are all clearly there in the biblical text, yet seldom does one see them "at work"—except in rare instances. One must ruefully admit that evangelical Christianity by and large does not expect much from God. He is given credit for all the ordinary things in our lives—as well He should be—but most Christians' expectation level, when it comes to the miraculous, is somewhere between zero and minus five. In fact, Dispensationalism and certain sectors of the Reformed tradition have circumvented all these texts with a theology that would leave the miraculous in the apostolic age. Even though evangelicals often pray, "If it be Thy will, please heal so-and-so," they would probably fall over in a dead faint if God actually answered their prayer.

The God of standard-brand evangelicalism is very much a God of the ordinary.

On the other hand, there is a way of interpreting these texts that can make a mockery of the divine will. "God promises us whatever we ask," is the battle cry. Fortunately, however, God does not grant everything we ask. For our asking is based on our own limited knowledge, and all too often it is colored by our self-interest. We can only praise God that He does not answer every prayer "prayed in faith." Hezekiah, after all, had his prayer answered and was granted fifteen more years, but it was during those years that Manasseh was born!

The real issue, therefore, when it comes to these texts, is not how "to get them to work for us," but how we are to understand them in the light of the full biblical revelation. How do they relate to the reality of God's sovereignty and His overall purposes with mankind? For the concerns of this paper, the crucial question is whether God specifically wills all Christians to know perfect health. If that were true, and there is not a text that supports it, then "failure" to be healed miraculously would indeed be a failure of our faith. But if it is not true, and it does not appear to be so, then faith not only believes specifically for healing, but also knows how to trust God when the effects of the Fall continue to be very much with us.

2. As with its "wealth" counterpart, the "gospel" of perfect health is also guilty of hermeneutical selectivity. Only those texts are selected which fit the scheme, and a whole series of hermeneutical gymnastics is devised to evade or explain away the texts that are an embarrassment to it.

Tied to this is the insistence on conventional wisdom as biblical. It is argued that every child of God *should* enjoy perfect health simply because he or she is a child of God; if they do *not* experience healing, then, of course, it is due to their lack of genuine trust in God. All of this simply refuses to take the Bible, the Fall, or common grace seriously. From their perspective Christ has redeemed us from the curse, therefore these evangelists will not allow the biblical view, which sees the Fall as permeating the whole fabric of the created order.

The Bible itself is much more realistic—and much more genuinely hopeful. God is revealed to have limitless power and resources; He regularly shows Himself strong on behalf of His people. Yet His people still live out their redeemed lives in a fallen world, where the whole creation, including the human body, is in "bondage to decay" (Romans 8:21), and will continue to be so until we receive "the redemption of our bodies" (8:23).

27

Thus the Bible records many of Elisha's miracles, including healings; yet quite matter-of-factly, without judgment, it also records that he "was suffering from the illness from which he died" (2 Kings 13:14). In a similar manner, it records that James was martyred and Peter delivered (Acts 12)—and Peter's deliverance was surely no direct result of his or the church's great faith!

Above all it is the Apostle Paul who presents problems for this point of view. On the one hand, his ministry was accompanied by "signs, wonders and miracles" (2 Corinthians 12:12; Romans 15:19); yet neither he nor his associates always experienced perfect health. And *never* is their sickness attributed to lack of faith, nor their recovery to great faith. Epaphroditus fell ill and nearly died, and in his case "God had mercy on him" (Philippians 2:26); yet Trophimus is left sick in Miletus (2 Timothy 4:20). For the sake of his frequent stomach disorders, Paul does *not* tell Timothy to pray or exercise faith for his healing. Again very matter-of-factly, he urges him to take wine for his sickness (1 Timothy 5:23). Why is it, one wonders, that the evangelists do not make *this* Scripture a part of their healing ministry?

Some have argued that in all these cases, and especially the latter, Paul was exhibiting a lack of faith. But such an approach must be vigorously resisted, because it means to sit in judgment on the Holy Spirit Himself. If we believe all of Scripture to be inspired of the Spirit, then *He* inspired "wine for the stomach" in Timothy's case, just as He inspired the laying on of hands and oil in James 5:14- 15.

More troublesome yet are Paul's own physical illnesses and sufferings. His own body was weak, or sickly (2 Corinthians 10:10). Indeed, he says he always carried about in his body the death of

Jesus (2 Corinthians 4:11), and the context makes it clear that he is referring to his bodily weaknesses. Outwardly he groaned (4:16), longing to replace his present earthly tent with the heavenly dwelling (5:1-2). He preached in Galatia as a direct result of illness (Galatians 4:12-15), which almost certainly was some kind of ailment of the eye. Whether or not this was also his "thorn in the flesh" (2 Corinthians 12:7), there can be little question that the problem for which he thrice sought deliverance was a physical one. Some, to be sure, have suggested that the "flesh" here is Paul's sinful nature and that some "person" (=messenger) from Satan was attacking his sinful tendencies. But that is to play havoc not only with this text and its context, but also with Paul's theology of life in the Spirit (Galatians 5; Romans 8).

The most common way to "get around" these texts has been to argue for a distinction between suffering and sickness. Suffering is something external to us, which comes as the result of our following Christ. This, it is argued, is what Paul suffered, and we may expect to as well. Sickness and disease, on the other hand, are a part of the Fall and the curse, and these have now been overcome by Christ.

But this is a distinction that cannot be sustained biblically. It is not that the biblical writers did not, or could not, know the differences; they simply do not make such distinctions. The clearest evidence of this is the fact that in both the Old and New Testaments the most common word for sickness is in fact the word *weakness*, so that frequently only the context alone tells us what kind of "weakness" is involved. (Compare for example, the differences in the NIV and the NASB on 2 Kings 1:2-3.)

29

The obvious reason for this usage is that *all* evil is seen to be the result of the Fall, not just sickness. And God can and does deliver from all evil, not just sickness. But in neither case does He always so deliver. Just as Satan was responsible for Paul's "thorn in the flesh," so also Paul was hindered by Satan from returning to Thessalonica (1 Thessalonians 2:18), yet there is no hint in either case that he or God "failed." Sickness, therefore, is not some unique part of the Fall, deliverance from which is ours on demand; it is simply a part of the whole of fallenness. We are promised healing; yet there is also a place in the present age for "a little wine" for one's frequent ailments.

3. The third area of weakness in the biblical interpretation of this movement is closely related to what has just been said. It is the failure to have, or to construct, an adequate biblical theology.

The essential framework of New Testament theology is eschatological; that is, it has to do with the coming of the End. By the time of the coming of Jesus, Jewish hopes for salvation had become totally eschatological. The present age was seen as under Satan's dominion, and thus totally evil. Evil men ruled, and they oppressed the righteous. The Jews had therefore come to give up on any salvation within history. They looked for God to vindicate them by bringing an end to the present age; He would do this through His Messiah, who would judge evil and usher in the New Age, the Kingdom of God.

It was into this kind of hope that Jesus came. He announced the Kingdom as present in His own ministry and proceeded to demonstrate it by healing the sick, casting out demons, and freely accepting the outcasts. Eschatological excitement reached fever pitch. But instead of ushering in the glorious New Age of their expectations, Jesus was crucified—and the lights went out.

But no, there was a glorious sequel. He was raised from the dead. Surely now is the time for the Kingdom, his disciples thought. But instead, He returned to the Father and sent the promised Holy Spirit. Right here is where the problems come in, both for the early church and for us. Jesus announced the coming Kingdom as having arrived with His own coming. The Spirit's coming in fullness and power were also signs that the New Age had arrived. Yet the End of this age apparently had not yet taken place. Evil and its effects are still very much in evidence. How were they to reconcile this?

Very easily, beginning with Peter's sermon in Acts 3, the church came to realize that Jesus had not come to usher in the "final" End, but the "beginning" of the End, as it were. Thus they came to see that with Jesus' death and resurrection, and with the coming of the Spirit, the blessings and benefits of the Future had already come. In a sense, therefore, the End had already come. But in another sense it had not yet fully come. Thus they saw the Kingdom, and salvation, as both *already* and *not yet*.

The early believers, therefore, saw themselves as a truly eschatological people, who lived "between the times"—that is, between the time of the beginning of the End and the consummation of the End. At the Lord's Table, they celebrated their eschatological existence by proclaiming "the Lord's death until he comes" (1 Corinthians 11:26). *Already* they knew God's free and full forgiveness, but they had *not yet* been perfected (Philippians 3:7-14). Already death was theirs (1 Corinthians 3:22), yet

31

they would still die (Philippians 3:20-22). Already they lived in the Spirit, yet they still lived in the world where Satan could attack. Already they had been justified and faced no condemnation, yet there was still to be a future judgment. They were God's "future people." They had been conditioned by the future; they knew its benefits, lived in light of its values. But they still had to live out these benefits and values in the present world.

The problem in Corinth, and that which the wealth and health gospel is repeating, was to emphasize the "already" in such a way that they almost denied the continuing presence of the world. They saw Christ only as exalted, but not as crucified. They believed that the only thing that glorified God was signs and wonders and power. Because God heals, He must heal everyone. There is no place for weakness or hunger or thirst for this kind of eschatological existence.

This false theology lay at the very heart of the Corinthian rejection of Paul. His bodily weaknesses did not commend him to their view of apostleship. An apostle should be "spiritual," eloquent, living in glory and perfect health. They rejected Paul and his theology of the cross (with its ongoing suffering in the present age), because they saw themselves as "spiritual," redeemed from such weakness. In their view Paul looked like anything but an apostle of their "glorious" Jesus.

Paul tries everything in his power to get them back to his gospel. In I Corinthians 1:18-25, he reminds them that the gospel has as its very base a "crucified Messiah." For the Corinthians that's like saying "fried ice." Messiah means power, glory, miracles; crucifixion means weakness, shame, suffering. Thus they gladly accepted the false apostles, who preached a "different Gospel" with "another Jesus" (2 Corinthians 11:4), and condemned Paul for his bodily weakness (10:10).

In 1 Corinthians 4:8-13 he tried irony. "Already you have all you want! Already you have come into your kingdom—and without us!" he tells them. Then, with absolutely brilliant strokes, he annihilates them with the stark contrasts between himself and them, with himself as the example of what it means to live out the future in the present age.

In 2 Corinthians 3-6, he tries to explain the true nature of apostleship, which has a glorious message but is proclaimed by a less-than-glorious messenger. "We have this treasure in jars of clay to show that this all-surpassing power is from God and not from us," he explains (4:7).

Finally, in 2 Corinthians 10-13, he attacks their false teachers head-on. To do so he plays the role of the "fool" as in the ancient dramas. Paul is forced to boast (because of his opponents), so in what does he boast? In all the very things the Corinthians are against—Paul's weaknesses. In total irony he finally sets himself alongside the boasts of the false apostles, with their great visions and miracle-stories. However—in keeping with his point—his vision turns out to have no great word of revelation (12:4; he was not even allowed to tell its content!), and his miracle story had no miracle! All of this because he was a true disciple of the Crucified One. God's strength is perfected *not* in His delivering His Messiah *from* crucifixion, nor in delivering His apostle *from* physical suffering, but is seen *in* the crucifixion *itself*, and *in* the apostle's weaknesses.

Thus the "perfect health" evangelists simply repeat the Corinthian error. They find it impossible to live in the tension between the already and the not yet. Because God has already brought the Kingdom, they demand all of the future in the present age—except for the final resurrection.

But 1 and 2 Corinthians stand over against this *over*-realized eschatology of theirs. Paul lived out a free, joyous existence in the already (in both want and plenty, in both sickness and health), because he knew that God had secured his life for the future—even though it was not yet fully realized. "Death is ours," Paul says, yet we still die. So with healing. It is ours; yet our bodies are not yet perfected. And in this present age, even some of God's choicest servants continue to be perfected through suffering, as was the Son of God Himself (Hebrews 5:8-9).

4. A final theological word. Again, as with the wealth side of their "gospel," the preaching of perfect health tends to put the *emphas'is* on the wrong *syllab'le*. Healing ultimately resides in God, they will affirm. Yet in actual practice, it is the result of man's faith. Indeed, they see God as under obligation to us in this matter.

Healing, therefore, instead of being a gracious expression of God's unlimited grace, is something He *has* to do—at our bidding. By way of contrast, the first sentence of a sound biblical theology may well be, God *must* do *nothing*. God is free to be God. He is sovereign in all things and is simply not under our control. The second sentence of a sound biblical theology will be: Although God *must* do *nothing*, in grace He does *all things*. No healing has ever been deserved; it is always an expression of God's grace. Some have asked, If God must do nothing, then why pray at all? Why not simply wait for Him to act sovereignly? The answer is simple: Because God answers prayer. The mystery of faith is that there is a wonderful correlation between our asking and trusting, and what goes on about us. God doesn't have to answer prayer, but He does. God doesn't have to heal, but He graciously does. Healing, therefore is not a divine obligation; it is a divine gift. And precisely because it is a gift, we can make no demands. But we can *trust* Him to do all things well!

THE NEW TESTAMENT VIEW OF WEALTH AND POSSESSIONS

Historically the church has repeatedly had to wrestle with its existence as a pilgrim people in an alien, temporal society. This has been true especially of its attitude toward wealth and material goods. For the first two Christian centuries that struggle was relatively easy. Christians, by and large, stood over against culture on this matter. When the emperor adopted the faith, however, the struggle began in earnest. The monastic movement was one of the direct results. Subsequent history has been an ebb and flow of accommodation and rejection. From time to time accommodation has brought guilt, which in turn caused some to construct a theology for rejection, while others constructed a theology to justify wholesale accommodation.

This historic struggle is currently an existential reality for American Christianity. In recent years the economic situation has increased wealth for most Americans on a grand scale, producing considerable tension for large numbers of American Christians—especially in light of the biblical mandate to care for the poor and the fact that one and a half billion people in today's world are malnourished. Most affluent American Christians have accommodated rather easily to an affluent life style, without giving it much thought. Others have sensed the tremendous disparity between their affluent circumstances and the lowly Nazarene, whose perfect humanity is seen as a model for us, and have opted for a simpler way of life. Still others have begun to argue that affluence is God's intention—His perfect will for His children.

My interest in this essay is not to try to resolve these tensions for the individual Christian in modern American society. Rather it is my hope to indicate what the New Testament itself teaches about wealth and material goods, so as to provide a biblical frame of reference for discussion and decision making.

Anyone with even a surface acquaintance with the New Testament has come to recognize that the Christian faith is decidedly on the side of "the poor" and that "the rich" seem regularly to "come in for it." Thus Jesus says, "Blessed are you who are poor" and "woe to you who are rich" (Luke 6:20, 24, NIV). His messianic credentials are vindicated by the fact that "the good news is preached to the poor" (Matt. 11:5; see Luke 4:18), while of the rich He says, "It is easier for a camel to go through the eve of a needle than for a rich man to enter the kingdom of God" (Mark 10:25). In his parable of the Sower He warns of "the deceitfulness of wealth and the desire for other things" that choke out the Word of God (Mark 4:19), while elsewhere He says that one cannot serve God and money—they are mutually exclusive masters (Matt. 6:24).

Such an attitude toward wealth is reflected further in James and Paul, not to mention John's Revelation (18:16-17: "Woe, Woe,

O great city, dressed in fine linen, purple and scarlet, and glittering with gold, precious stones and pearls! In one hour such great wealth has been brought to ruin"). James shames the church for showing favoritism to the rich (2:1-7) and especially in 5:1-6 condemns the rich for their oppression of the poor ("Now listen, You rich people, weep and wail because of the misery that is coming up on you"). And Paul warns that the rich who eat their "lovefeasts" and Lord's Supper with regard to the poor are coming under God's judgment (1 Cor. 11:17-34): elsewhere he warns those who want to get rich that such people "fall into temptation and a trap and into many foolish and harmful desires that plunge men into ruin and destruction" (1 Tim. 6:6-10).

In the light of such texts it is no wonder that affluent Christians sometimes experience guilt, as though wealth, or being wealthy, in itself were evil. But such is not the case. As we shall see, it is the abuse or accumulation of wealth while others are in need that is called into question.

It is possible of course, to argue—as some have—that these texts merely reflect the sociology of the early Christians, whose Founder was a peasant carpenter, and whose early adherents were "not many wise, nor influential, nor of noble birth" (1 Cor. 1:26) and who had sometimes experienced the confiscation of their property (Heb. 10:34). Blessing the poor and condemning the rich was simply their form of making a virtue of necessity.

But such a sociological reading of the New Testament is a thorough misunderstanding of the deeply theological motivation of New Testament ethics, which ultimately derives from the Old Testament revelation of God as the One who Himself champions the cause of the poor.

It should be noted here that "the poor" in both the New and especially the Old Testaments, refers not merely to those in economic poverty. The "poor" are the powerless, the disenfranchised, those whose situation forces them to be dependent on the help of others. Thus it includes especially the widow and the orphan, as well as the alien, and even the Levite. The Old Testament Law, therefore, is filled with statutes that protect such people from the aggrandizement of the powerful, who of course are people with authority—and money

Interestingly enough, it has been the Old Testament that has often been seen as the "balance" to the New with regard to personal wealth and prosperity. For here indeed one regularly finds prosperity (especially lands and children) as evidence of God's favor (e.g., Deut. 28:14; Psalm 112:1-3; 128:1-4). So much is this so that Sir Francis Bacon could write: "Prosperity is the blessing of the Old Testament; adversity is the blessing of the New."

But what is often overlooked in such texts is that they are invariably tied to the concepts of God's righteousness and justice. It is only as one is righteous—i.e., walks in accordance with God's Law—that one is promised the blessing of abundance and family. But to be righteous meant especially that one cared for, or pleaded the cause of, the poor and the oppressed.

Such a concern is so thoroughgoing in the Old Testament that it is found in its every strata and expression: Law, Narrative, Poetry, Wisdom, Prophet.

Thus in the so-called Book of the Covenant (Exod. 21-23), right in the midst of laws about seducing a virgin, sex with animals, practicing magic, and sacrificing to foreign gods, Israel is told not to mistreat or oppress an alien (22:21) and not to take advantage of a widow or an orphan (22:22). If they do the latter, they are warned, "My anger will be aroused, and I will kill you with the sword; your wives will become widows and your children fatherless" (22:23-24). In the same context they are commanded to lend to the poor without interest and to return a poor man's coat taken in pledge by sundown, because "I am compassionate." In Exodus 23:10-11, the Sabbath year was instituted expressly for the poor, as was the Jubilee year in Leviticus 25 and 27.

This same concern for the disenfranchised is thoroughgoing in Deuteronomy (e.g., 10:17-19; 15:1-4, 7-11; 24:14-22; 27:19) and in the Psalter, which especially extols God because He cares for the poor and comes to their rescue (e.g., 9:8-9, 12, 18; 10:9-14, 17-18; 12:5; 22:24-26; 35:10; 68:4-5, 10). In the great messianic Psalm 72, the "royal son" above all else, "will judge your afflicted ones with justice" (v. 2); "He will defend the afflicted among the people and save the children of the needy" (v. 4; see vv. 12-14).

Precisely because God *is* like this, and His Anointed One *will be* like this (see Isa. 11:4; 42:1-4; 61:1), it is required of His people that they too plead the cause of the poor. This is especially true of those in authority. Thus it is only after he has murdered and stolen Naboth's vineyard that God's final judgment is pronounced on Ahab (2 Kings 21); and a strong part of Job's defense of his own righteousness was that he had in fact cared for the Poor (29:11-17; 31:16-23).

All of this comes to its focal point in the prophets, whose condemnation of Israel repeatedly has three elements: idolatry, sexual immorality, and injustice to the poor (see Exod. 22:21-27 above). It is because "they sell into slavery honest men who cannot pay their debts, poor men who cannot even repay the price of a pair of sandals" (Amos 2:6-7 GNB), and because they "twist justice and cheat people out of their rights" and "prevent the poor from getting justice in the courts" (5:7, 12) that God condemns Israel (see Isa. 1:17, 23; 3:15; 5:8, 23; 58:1-12; Micah 2:1-2, 8-9; 3:1-4, 11; 6:8-12; Zech. 7:8-14; and many, many others).

Righteousness in the Old Testament, therefore, calls for fair treatment of the poor. This is the way God is; this is the righteousness He demands. The poor are not to receive better things, or to be treated differently, but to be treated justly—and mercifully. Since the powerful and wealthy controlled the judges, the poor had only God to plead their cause. Thus it is not surprising that in messianic passages the needs of the poor are going to receive God's special attention.

It is within such a context of "fulfillment" that one must view the ministry of Jesus. But there is an added dimension. With Him the Kingdom of God had made its appearance. This meant for Him—and the early Christians—that in His own person and ministry the messianic age, the "blessedness" of the future, had dawned in human history. Jesus, therefore, is the beginning of the End, the inauguration of God's final rule. Thus He came with good news for the poor, which for Jesus meant not only the time of justice for the economically deprived, the vulnerable, but also the time of the gracious acceptance and forgiveness of sinners.

Precisely because with Him the New Age had dawned, this meant that the overthrow of the old order with its old values and injustices had begun. Because God's Rule had come, people were freed from the tyranny of self-rule and the need "to get ahead." One cannot serve God and Mammon. Because God accepts and secures us, we need no longer be anxious about material things (Matt: 6:24-34). And because God thus accepts and secures us, we can freely sell our possessions and give to the needy (Luke 12:32-34) and freely love our enemies and lend to them without expecting to get anything back (Luke 6:32-36). Indeed, the apostle John later says, if one has material possessions and cares nothing for the poor, such a person knows nothing of God's love (1 John 3:17-18: see 4:19-21).

It is within this twofold framework—the revelation of God as the One who brings justice to the poor and the inauguration of God's Rule in the ministry of Jesus—that we must view the New Testament texts on money and possessions. Poverty *per se* is not being glorified, nor is wealth condemned. In the new age a whole new order has been inaugurated, with a new way of looking at things and a new value system.

It is clear that Jesus sees possessions in the old age as doing the possessing, not being possessed. Possessions tend to tyrannize or lead to a false security. Hence some of His strongest words move in this direction. "Woe to the rich, the full," He says (Luke 6:24-26), not because there is evil in wealth, but alas, because the rich "already have received their comfort." They see themselves as "in need of nothing," including God. Like the rich fool, they seek more and more because they think life consists in having a surplus of possessions. but they are "not rich toward God" (Luke 12:13-21).

"How hard it is for a rich man to enter the Kingdom," Jesus says. Indeed, it is easier for a camel to go through the eye of a needle. Jesus' point is that it takes a miracle for the rich to be saved, because they are secure in their possessions.

But it is equally clear that Jesus did not have an ascetic's eye toward property. If He had "no place to lay His head" (Luke 9:58), He and His disciples were in fact supported by the means of well-to-do women (Luke 8:2f.); and Peter owned a home in Capernaum to which Jesus repaired. In reflecting on the fourth commandment, He says that parents are to be supported from their children's possessions (Mark 7:9-13). In requiring money to be lent without hope of return there is the presupposition of money. Jesus went to dinners with the rich as well as the poor.

Zaccheus was not required to give up all his possessions: that he made a surplus reparation was the evidence of his salvation.

All of this is true because for Jesus wealth and possessions were a zero value. In the new age they simply do not count. The standard is sufficiency: and surplus is called into question. The one with two tunics should share with him who has none (Luke 3:11); "possessions" are to be sold and given to the poor (Luke 12:33). Indeed, in the new age *unshared wealth* is contrary to the Kingdom breaking in as good news to the poor. Thus, as Martin Hengel has so eloquently put it:

> Jesus was not interested in any new theories about the rightness or wrongness of possessions in themselves, about the origin of property or its better distribution; rather he adopted the same scandalously free and untrammelled attitude to property as to the powers of the state, the alien Roman rule and its Jewish confederates. The imminence of the kingdom of God robs all these things of their power de facto, for in it "many that are first will be last, and the last first" (Mark 10:31; Matthew 19:30, 20:16; Luke 13:30). Of course, Jesus attacks mammon with the utmost severity where it has captured men's hearts, because this gives it demonic character by which it blinds men's eyes to God's will—in concrete terms, to their neighbour's needs. Mammon is worshipped wherever men long for riches, are tied to riches, keep on increasing their possessions and want to dominate as a result of them *(Property and Riches in the Early Church* [Fortress, 1974], p.30).

It is precisely this new age attitude that one also finds reflected in the early chapters of the Acts. The early church was *not* communal. But it was the new community—the new people of God. Hence no one considered anything owned to be his own possession. The coming of the Spirit that marked the beginning of the new order had freed them from the need of possessing. Hence there was sufficiency, and no one was in need.

This same carefree attitude toward wealth and possessions also marks all of Paul. He is a free man in Christ, who knows contentment whatever the circumstances. He knows both want and plenty, both hunger and being well fed. He "can do all things"—which in this context clearly refers to being in need!—"through Christ who gives him strength" (Phil. 4:10-13).

Thus he tells those who have nothing to be content with food and clothing: "People who *want to get rich* fall into temptation and a trap" (1 Tim. 6:6-10). But then he remembers those who *happen to be rich*. They are to treat their wealth with indifference: they must not put any stock in it. Rather they are to be "generous and willing to share," for this is true wealth (6:17-19).

It seems to me that this is the biblical framework within which American Christianity must once again begin to move and have its being. For many of us this will mean the adoption of a simpler way of life—not as Law, but as gratitude to Grace. For many it will also mean courage—courage to withstand the paganism of our materialistic culture and courage to give time and money to "unpopular causes," such as prison reform and world poverty. Such programs as Bread for the World, John Perkin's Voice of Calvary in Mississippi, the Catholic Worker Movement, and Charles Colson's Prison Fellowship are leading the way for us in these matters. God's call to us is for a return to biblical faith and to a radical obedience to our Lord Jesus Christ. This does not require poverty, but it does require righteousness, which in this context means to use our wealth not to manipulate others, but to alleviate the hurt and pain of the oppressed.

Printed in the United States
69506LVS00006B/13